Be Your Own Financial Planner

by

Homer W. Worrell

DORRANCE
PUBLISHING CO
EST. 1920
PITTSBURGH, PENNSYLVANIA 15238

Dorrance Publishing Co
585 Alpha Drive
Suite 103
Pittsburgh, PA 15238
Visit our website at www.dorrancebookstore.com

ISBN: 978-1-6453-0226-1
eISBN: 978-1-6453-0852-2

Contents

Overview

Half of Americans Have Little Chance for Financial Freedom

A lesson learned over 22 years of financial planning experience was that half of all Americans cannot afford financial services. They are deserving of financial freedom but do not have the resources to afford financial planning fees or the cost of brokered financial products. This situation is not satisfactory and the reason for writing this book. Here is a simple do-it-yourself guide to seek financial freedom in your lifetime. You get to achieve all below without the planning cost:

- Complete your own Professional Financial Plan
- Choose and buy your own financial products of investment and insurance
- Implement your financial plan
- Review your success to achieving financial freedom
- Save thousands of dollars on advisor costs and product costs.

So simple and easy to follow, almost everyone can master!

Starting a financial plan involves relatively simple steps. Yet, as the plan matures and more money is accumulated, the steps to continued planning become more complex. For example, required minimum distributions from a plan are not required until age 70½. Greater diversification in the portfolio is not necessary until additional assets are accumulated. At some point in the do-it-yourselfer's investing life, hiring a financial planner will be needed to efficiently manage assets. This writing is simple and designed for beginning investors who want to get ahead financially. Understand that delays in starting your investment will not fully utilize the time value of money. So, for the first years of investing, we will save the cost of financial planning and brokered financial products by being our own financial advisor.

Many Americans do not use a financial advisor either for lack of trust in general or they cannot afford the cost of an advisor. Statistics show that 24% of all Americans do not use an advisor for lack of trust. Yet, in either case, for lack of money or lack of advisor trust, having the ability to be your own advisor and do–it–yourself is a workable early stage solution for achieving financial freedom. The goal is financial freedom. Finding a good method to accomplish financial planning for Americans who cannot or will not invest is the objective of this book.

Numerous attempts have been made to provide a do-it-yourself guide for financial planning. Yet these attempts have not provided enough simplicity, how-to, or completeness. So Americans simply don't use them and seek something better. Now better is here. The do-it-yourself investor can afford this strategy and will save thousands of dollars in investment costs over a lifetime, enable the personal preparation of a workable financial plan, and give their family an opportunity for financial freedom.

Discover simple step-by-step guidance on how to do financial planning, how to select and purchase financial products, how to implement the plan, and how to review and update the plan on a yearly basis. This work can lead to financial freedom.

Simplicity is the key. Financial planning can be very complex, but it does not have to be this way in the beginning years. The number of products can be overwhelming, but we will focus on those financial products that are easiest to understand and can produce success in achieving financial freedom. Our real focus is to provide an opportunity for lower-income Americans to have a financial plan without the high planning and product cost. A college degree is not required. The average person who can reason and who works hard can do this. Look at these characteristics and see if they fit you.

- Ability to save regularly no matter how small

- Willingness to invest
- Have time to invest
- Have discipline to invest
- Have confidence in personal ability
- Ability to set goals
- Will review details and apply best practice

Do these characteristics fit you? If so, read on. If not, seek a refund of this book.

Hiring a financial planner and buying brokered financial products can cost thousands of dollars. For many this is unaffordable. Brokered funds offered by financial planners with sales charges are on par regarding performance and profitability with no-load mutual funds, which are offered at no sales charge to the buying public. This begs the question, why buy brokered funds? Saving sales charges and advisor fees and doing the work yourself is an affordable way to begin the quest for financial freedom. We intend to show you a way to be your own advisor.

Preface

Seek Financial Freedom with this Book

This book was written for Americans who cannot afford a financial planner, about 50 percent of all Americans. The best approach to financial freedom is hiring a professional financial planner. Yet, too many cannot afford one. Congratulations to Americans who are wealthy enough to afford financial planning. You don't need to buy this book. It was expressly written to help lower-income American who cannot afford the high cost of financial planning. When your yearly income is below $35k per year, family resources are required to provide for the necessities of life with little money remaining to invest. Moreover, the lower half of the middle-income class, $35k to $75k, have dollars to invest but, the dollars are usually devoted to company-sponsored retirement plans that provide matching funds like the Thrift Savings Plan (TSP) or the company 401(k). These retirement plans do not involve a financial advisor or the cost of financial planning. When used alone, they do not produce financial freedom.

Roughly half of all Americans have no good chance to achieve financial freedom in their lifetime due to low family income levels and financial planning cost. There has to be a solution for these Americans. Agree? Income levels can be improved through individual effort, and the cost of investing can be reduced. Can this reduction in investing cost help solve this lack of financial freedom? The answer is a resounding YES! This book details a no-cost, do-it-yourself strategy for financial planning. It drastically reduces the cost of quality financial products through direct insurance and discount mutual funds, no-load mutual funds, and index mutual funds. Read on; this book will tell you and show you how to be a "do–it–yourself" financial planner and investor.

Book Cover Message

The book cover shows a beautiful arched rainbow over a forested hillside. Rich green trees and some poor brown dying trees cover the landscape. The trees on the cover are symbolic of the American population of wealthy and not so wealthy people. The rainbow symbolizes the opportunity for wealth. Folklore says there is a pot of gold at the end of every rainbow. One must just locate the rainbow's end to enjoy the riches. However, the rainbow is a mirage and has no end and no pot of gold. Too many Americans, like the dying brown trees, count on luck or lottery to achieve financial freedom. Yet, Financial freedom is not folklore, it is real and achievable. Read and implement this book and find your pot of gold.

Important Note

The example plan in this book is not a recommendation to purchase listed financial products rather, it is simply a sample plan that shows the reader example plan components that are required.

Chapter 1

Do-It-Yourself Strategy

It is important to give the opportunity of financial freedom to Americans who cannot fully invest because of income level, those Americans earning $75k per year or less. A major reason these Americans cannot invest is the high cost of investing. Why attempt to do your own financial planning? Simply to avoid high planning costs. Most lower-income Americans have discretionary money. However, this discretionary money is not invested. We find these monies in bank savings accounts, under the mattress, or in a buried tin can in the backyard. These places are where the money cannot grow and assist the lower-income Americans to achieve financial independence. Investments are a better place to keep these funds.

Who are these lower-income Americans? They are the backbone of the American working class. High school and college graduates usually go to work soon after graduation to earn a living and take their rightful place in society. In the early working years, their income level is under $75k. This places the young working class in our target market. We will call them millennials. As their income rises above $75k per year in their latter working years, they can transition into the class of Americans that can afford an advisor to assist in their quest for financial freedom. Our next target group is Americans in the working class that will not earn more than $75k per year in all their working years. Our two-target markets for the do-it-yourself financial planning approach are:

1. Young working-class Americans, millennials, earning less than $75k per year.
2. Other working-class Americans that will earn less than $75k per year in their working lifetime.

How many Americans belong to these two groups? About 50 percent of the American population, or roughly 163,000,000 Americans. Do these Americans deserve the opportunity for financial freedom? **Absolutely.** So why not just allow group 1 to reach the $75k income level, then begin investing through an advisor? The answer is time. Time is probably the most significant aspect of investing to achieve financial freedom. A working lifetime starts as early as 18 years old after graduation from high school and ends with retirement around age 65 for a total of 47 working years. The example below will highlight the value of time in achieving financial freedom:

- $500/ month invested for 47 years, earning 8 percent per year, grows to **$3,126,896.**
- $500/ month invested for 37 years, earning 8 percent per year, grows to **$1,367,254.**

In this example, you can see that waiting just 10 years to start investing can cost you 56 percent less than investing for the entire 47 years. Time is an all-important consideration in investing.

Some believe that financial planning is an expertise reserved for the highly educated, very intelligent professionals. Not so fast. Earning financial advisor status does not require a college degree. Advisors take examinations for licensing and upon passing the exams they are legal to practice financial planning. These examinations can be taken multiple times until passed. Regular people with high school diplomas have the ability to perform the art. Having and using this "how-to" publication makes simplistic financial planning doable. Personal skills and tools are required. Below is a sample listing of skills that do-it-yourself planners should possess:

1. Basic mathematic skills
2. Attention to detail
3. Reasoning ability

4. Computer skills
5. Reading skills
6. Motivation to achieve financial freedom
7. Normal intelligence
8. Writing ability

Tools needed to perform do-it-yourself financial planning and investing:

1. Computer with printer
2. Internet
3. Calculator
4. Compound interest tables
5. Paper and pen

Shockingly, the reader can see that an average person with non-sophisticated skills and tools can perform financial planning.

So, the real question is, can our target groups of Americans be successful using a do-it-yourself approach to financial planning and investing? The answer is a resounding **yes**, but read on. We are going to provide a simple step-by-step guide to produce your own financial plan, fund it, and evaluate it.

Chapter 2

Preparing Your Own Financial Plan

History shows us that unless something changes, you will continue to receive the same result. In this case, without this publication with implementation, too many Americans get the same result: inadequate financial resources in retirement. Follow this book, then enjoy a financially rewarding retirement. Relying on social security alone is sure to disappoint the family in retirement. Start your retirement plan now. Just do it!

Your own financial plan will include these seven easy steps:

1. Benchmark your current financial reality. Prepare a budget for your current expenditures by using the budget form provided in plan tools. Compute your current monthly income from all sources. Compare your expenditure total to the current income. The result is the amount of money remaining after you have met monthly obligations. Occasionally, the numbers are somewhat shocking. Some Americans cannot determine where their money is spent. As a result, we cannot account for all the monthly income spent. Should this situation occur, stop this plan now. We will need to do some budget work, discussed at the end of this chapter. For those that can account for the monies spent, we can determine the surplus or shortage of dollars available for planning. When a shortage of dollars exists, stop this planning now. We will need to manage resources differently to produce a surplus. Again, we will address the shortage of dollars at the end of this chapter.

With a surplus of dollars determined, decisions can be made as to how the surplus will be spent. Naturally, devoting all or a major portion of these dollars to financial freedom can fund the financial plan. Next, we will review financial documents of existing investments and evaluate the quality/retainability of each investment. When your current investment is performing well, keep it. When the investment is not performing well, and the risk comparisons between your risk profile and the investment do not match, consider replacement or transfer of the investment. Choosing an appropriate investment starts with determination of investment objective. Popular investment objectives are growth, income, or both. However, for our purposes the growth objective is preselected as the appropriate investment objective. Americans that have not invested will require growth of assets to achieve an adequate nest egg in retirement.

2. Complete the risk questionnaire and compute results. (The questionnaire and result key are in plan tools.) Investment models that will match an individual's risk tolerance are combinations of bond mutual funds and equity mutual funds. See plan tools for the models that are appropriate for your risk tolerance. When the breadwinner and spouse have widely different risk tolerances, family negotiation should be performed to select a family planning risk tolerance to use.

3. Determine long term goals (with spouse). For many Americans the goals will include a check a month in retirement, home paid for, college paid for children and more. Record the goals and year for accomplishment. Know that long-term investing is a journey and not a race. Trading frequently is for the short-term investor and usually detrimental for the long-term investor. Be a long-term investor. Use the compound interest tables in plan tools to project the impact of 3% inflation per year. Simply multiply the amount of the goal times the multiplier in the compound interest tables. If you prefer, use an interest calculator on the internet to perform this calculation. Total the future amounts for all goals and you have determined the target retirement goal for accomplishment.

4. Evaluate risk. This exercise is more meaningful for couples versus single Americans. Financial freedom takes a lifetime to achieve.

Therefore, premature loss of a loved one, especially the breadwinner, is devastating, eliminating the opportunity of financial freedom for a surviving spouse. Consider transferring this potential loss of income to insurance. In addition, significant loss of property or lawsuit could severely lessen the opportunity for financial freedom. Home loss is a good example. When this review is complete, decisions can then be made on which values of potential losses should be mitigated and transferred to insurance.

5. Determine plan recommendations. Select at least one mutual fund per financial goal and the insurance product(s) that will solve the risk(s) determined to mitigate. Further, ensure that investments consider tax registered mutual funds. The check-a-month goal and the home purchase goal in our example can be funded with mutual funds registered as Individual Retirement Accounts (IRAs). Investments growing tax free, like a Roth IRA, earn more money for the investor due to tax savings. Similarly, the college goal should be registered as a college savings plan, like a 529 college savings plan, to enjoy tax-free earnings. As monthly dollar investment input increases beyond the IRA contribution limit, additional registration and mutual funds are required to complete target goal funding. This selection process is the heart of financial planning. The ultimate objective is to find a match between products and planning criteria. In the financial industry, this action is called suitability. Planning criteria can be almost infinitum. Common criteria are listed below:

   a. Investor risk tolerance compared to product risk
   b. Possibility of goal achievement (project 8% growth per year/is there enough time?)
   c. Product effectiveness to goal achievement (know product characteristics)
   d. Investor characteristics (personal preferences and ability to fund plan)
   e. Risks to mitigate

The do-it-yourself planner is the person responsible for suitability in product selection. Poor selections will normally yield poor results. Give suitability your best effort.

6. Money contributions to the plan. Each product in the plan must be funded with lumpsum or monthly dollars or both to establish the investment. Mutual funds do have minimum funding level criteria, so monthly dollars must meet the minimum funding level for the mutual fund. Occasionally, current monthly dollars will not be enough to reach all future goals, so we must plan for future increases to the monthly amounts based on improvements to the monthly budget and the target funding requirements. At yearly review and update for this plan, future funding is executed. This future monthly funding sample can be used as an example:

Next monthly income increase	How much $	Source of increase $
3rd Quarter future year	100.00/month	Pay raise
1st Quarter future year	500.00/month	Spouse starts work

When other investment or savings are available, we can determine the suitability of these assets to our plan. Suitability is the guiding determinant to any transfer. This determination of suitability is difficult and may warrant the assistance of a professional.

7. Preparation of the plan: List the goals, timeline for accomplishment, and total value for accomplishment. Record insurance needed to mitigate selected risk. The example below has the elements needed in the plan. Simplicity is the key.

Paul and Susan Rocksteady and son, Jeffery: Paul is 35 years old, Susan is 30 years old, and son Jeffery is 5. Paul is a government worker earning $70k per year, or $5,800 per month. He has 15% of the monthly income available to devote to his financial plan. Currently, he invests $150 per month in TSP with matching funds. Current balance in TSP is $45,000. Susan is a stay-at-home mom. The family risk tolerance is moderately aggressive.

Financial Plan:
A. Investment
Goal 1. One-time purchase of dream home, cost 450,000, bought at Paul's age, 65.

Goal 2. Check-a-month of $2000 starting at Paul's age, 65.

Goal 3. College for Jeffery- 4 college years starting at age 19, for $30k per year, total $120,000.

Grand total for all goals is **$3,021,151** at Paul's age, 65 (example calculation follows plan recommendation).

B. Insurance

Replace the yearly income for Paul the breadwinner, should Paul die early. Make this calculation by computing the number of years need until goal accomplishment. In our example Paul is 35 and contribution to goals will continue until age 65. We must cover the family from age 35 until contributions to the plan are projected to end at 65. The coverage needed is yearly income of $70k times 30 years. Amount of insurance is $2,100,000 of 30-year level term insurance. For simplicity, we will round the insurance amount to two million. Family will not purchase final expense insurance at this time. Mortgage insurance on the current home is covered through the mortgage company with premium included in the mortgage payment.

Example Plan: TSP is suitable for the family and the plan recommends continuing this investment. Mutual fund selection and insurance selection are addressed in the next chapter but shown here to provide complete components.

A. Investment:

Goal 1: Schwab total stock market index fund, funded at $150 per month. Register as a Roth IRA in Paul's name.

Goal 2: Vanguard 500 index fund, funded at $150 per month. Register as a Roth IRA in Susan's name.

Goal 3: Fidelity 500 index investments, funded at $150 per month. Register as a 529 college savings plan in Jeffery's name.

Continue: TSP, funded at $150 per month.

B. Insurance:

$2,000,000 coverage of 30-year level term insurance with Lincoln National Insurance Company, cost is $154.70 per month.

Goal calculation in our example:

1. Home cost today is $450,000 times (the 3-percent yearly inflation rate) 2.427 (found in single-payment compound interest table) = $1,092,150 future home cost.
2. Today's $2,000 check a month in 30 years inflated at 3 percent = $4,854 per month. Therefore, future monthly amount of $4,854 times 30 years = $1,747,440 total future value.
3. College cost today is $120,000 ($30,000 per year for 4 years) times the 3% yearly inflation rate for 14 years = $181,560.

Home goal total	=	$ 1,092,150
Check-a-month total	=	$ 1,747,440
College goal total	=	$ 181,560
Total Goal	=	$3,021,151

Three million dollars accumulated within a 30-year period requires about $2000 invested per month at 8% growth rate. Therefore, the Rocksteady family will need to increase the monthly investment amount when the family can afford to do so. Investing an additional $450 per month with this plan and continuing the $150 per month to TSP is a good beginning. Stay flexible with your ability to invest. Goal projection elements of rate of return, time, and amount invested are variables. All money that you invest in financial planning for retirement will improve your retirement standard of living.

Americans who cannot account for monthly dollars spent cannot benefit from this book until budget accountability can be established. Preparing a budget is not difficult, but tracking expenditures and recording the expenditures to determine where dollars are spent will take time and discipline. My recommendation for Americans who face this challenge is to prepare a budget and record expenditures over a 6-month period. Upon success with this budget effort to accurately account for all monthly expenditures for 6 months, you can benefit from this guide.

For Americans that find the budget receipts and expenditures are co-equal or expenditures are greater than income, financial planning cannot proceed until monies are available to fund a financial plan. Earning more money, debt reduction, avoidance of impulse spending, and non-use of credit cards can be a way forward here.

Chapter 3

Selection of Financial Products
(Insurance and Mutual Funds)

Selection of investment products for the do-it-yourself financial planner should come from the families of no-load index mutual funds, no-load mutual funds, or discount mutual funds to achieve the lowest cost investment. Regarding insurance, we are trying to avoid commission cost by buying insurance from direct purchase insurance firms. Avoid buying insurance from a captive insurance agent, one who works for an insurance firm or financial planning firm. This will save commission cost. Remember, we are seeking the lowest cost for financial planning and products, allowing lower-income families to affordably invest. We have eliminated the financial planning cost of a financial advisor by doing it yourself. Now we shift our effort to low- or no-cost investments, and low-cost, no-commission insurance.

The "load" on the managed mutual fund means that the fund has a sales charge. Sales charges can be from zero to eight percent of invested amount. Brokered funds are the funds that have a sales charge or load. The load of the fund is paid to the broker. No-load mutual funds do not have a load. The broker is bypassed when the investor buys directly from the producer. So, if you want to save money? Avoid brokers and buy no-load mutual funds yourself. Discount loaded mutual funds are offered by a select few brokers and have dramatically reduced the sales charge. The discount mutual fund will have much less sales charge, like 3 percent. The absolute lowest cost of mutual funds available is the no-load index mutual funds. These funds are not managed, rather they are a cross section of a sector of stocks. For example, index funds can be found in the large cap stocks, small cap stocks, or international stocks. The cross section of stocks in the mutual fund does not change until a stock is added to or dropped from the index. A fund manager is not needed in this case. An example of index funds is the Thrift Savings Plan. It has a small cap, S-fund and large cap, C fund and an international, I fund. Since there is no management, there is no management fee. When choosing an index fund, the individual's risk tolerance is the guiding selection criteria. Concerning risk level, stocks are rated from lower to higher in this way.

Lower ————————————————— Higher
Large Cap— International— Small Cap

We are not complete without discussing exchange traded funds (ETFs). They are usually index funds with no load, but you must open a brokerage account and pay a brokerage fee to buy them. Trading is encouraged in ETFs much like stocks in the stock market. We are not recommending ETFs due to the brokerage cost involved and the tendency to trade frequently.

Operational expense ratio is the fee that includes management cost and overall expense of fund. Index funds will have the absolute lowest cost of all funds since there is no management and the operational cost is minimal. We are recommending that 100 percent of all investment for the do-it-yourself investor be made by buying no-load index funds. If you want to place managed funds in your portfolio, choose no more than 20 percent of your portfolio in managed funds. For example, if you have five funds in your portfolio, one fund can be managed. Select your index mutual funds by reviewing the top-rated no-load index funds on the internet. Considering your risk tolerance, find the funds that closely or precisely match your risk. Review the "Risk allocation model" in plan tools for assistance to make this match.

Managed mutual fund investment selection is not recommended and is considerably more difficult. Here, the investor will pay for fund management. These funds, if desired, should be selected from discount managed mutual funds to achieve the lowest cost. Select the fund based upon family risk tolerance assessment and the suitability of the investment for the investor. Selection of a good mutual fund can, in part, be made based upon ratings found on the internet. However, the determination of suitability for the investor requires consideration of many parameters like risk tolerance, price, goal timeline, management, and others. Determination of suitability will be the do-it-yourselfers most difficult task to perform. Selecting these funds from the top-rated funds of Money Line or Kiplinger is a good beginning, but don't stop there. Evaluate these characteristics:

1. Low Expenses
2. Strong Fund Manager
3. Consistent Investment Process
4. Strong Parent Company
5. Not too big (not important for Large Cap or Index)
6. Specific investment strategy to accomplish goal
7. Outstanding long-term rate of return
8. Member of published top mutual funds list

Below you find six index mutual funds that were extracted from the internet in January 2019 that meet our recommended criteria with 100% index fund selection:

Index Fund	Lifetime rate of return	Expense ratio	Ticker symbol
Equity			
Vanguard 500 index	11.17%	0.14	VFINX
Vanguard total stock market	9.90%	0.14	VTSMX
Fidelity 500 index	10.46%	0.15	FUSEX
Schwab total stock market	12.67%	0.03	SWTSX
Bond			
Vanguard total bond fund	5.75%	0.15	VBMFX
Fidelity total bond	4.61%	0.45	FTBFX

Selection of insurance products is next. Families can mitigate their risk by choosing term or permanent insurance. Term insurance is for temporary risk mitigation and permanent insurance is for permanent risk mitigation.

First, we must define the role that insurance will play in your financial plan. For almost all plans for the do-it-yourselfer, life insurance will mitigate the risk of premature death of the breadwinner, creating a cashflow to support survivors. This type of insurance is term insurance, probably a level term for 10, 20, or 30 years. Determining the amount of insurance is a function of the cash flow needed for the survivor. Final expenses are a permanent risk and the most effective product to mitigate this risk is permanent insurance. Low-cost whole life or guaranteed death benefit universal life will be your least expensive choice. Usually, the amount of insurance required for final expenses does not exceed $50k per person. Remember, we are mitigating the risk that the loss of the breadwinner will not allow completion of the investment piece of the plan. Life insurance is an expense, not an investment. Never consider insurance as an investment, as mutual funds are your best choice of products for wealth accumulation.

Property loss is the second reason to buy insurance. Here, home mortgage payoff is a leading issue. All mortgage companies will require insurance to cover your loan. Many times, mortgage insurance from the loan company is too expensive. Alternative insurance can be more cost effective. A low-cost level term insurance will suffice. When you have mortgage insurance, do some cost comparisons. If you are in the process of home purchase, choose to buy mortgage insurance yourself. These actions will insure your lowest insurance cost.

Choosing an insurance company is a process of surfing the internet of direct purchase insurance companies. Several are available, and the list is growing. Buying from a direct purchase insurance company can save the commission cost of buying from a captive insurance agent. Several quotes from different companies may be required to find the lowest-cost company for direct purchase. Sometimes an independent insurance agent can save time in this process. They occasionally have a listing of the lowest prices available from direct purchase firms. The process of buying direct from the insurance producer can take an extended time, as underwriting issues must be accomplished before the purchase can move forward. The highest-rated insurance carriers are your best choice. Companies are rated A to D. Always choose an A-rated company.

Lastly, don't make the mistake of ignoring risk mitigation in your financial plan. Many investors just don't think it through, as the effect of your death is not a pleasant thought. Yet your survivors are dependent on your consideration of this problem to have a reasonable lifestyle should you die early.

Searching for direct purchase insurance is a web-surfing exercise that can take some time. Get enough quotes to expose the lowest cost. Some sites like "Select Quote" will allow you to compare rates from several insurance companies. Then, an online application must be submitted for the insurance company chosen. After evaluation of the application, the insurance company will determine the rate category that will be offered. Buying direct purchase insurance can negate commission cost. This is one of our objectives for the do-it-yourself investor. Our example plan with product selection and registration are listed below:

Example Plan: TSP is suitable for the family and the plan recommends continuing this investment.

A. Investment.
   Goal 1: Schwab total stock market index fund, funded at $150 per month. Register as a Roth IRA in Paul's name.
   Goal 2: Vanguard 500 index fund, funded at $150 per month. Register as a Roth IRA in Susan's name.
   Goal 3: Fidelity 500 index fund, funded at $150 per month. Register as a 529 college savings plan in Jeffery's name.
   Continue: TSP, funded at $150 per month.
B. Insurance: $2,000,000 coverage of 30-year level term insurance with Lincoln National Insurance Company, cost is $154.74 per month.

Chapter 4

Implementing Your Plan

Implementation follows completion of your do-it-yourself financial plan and selection of your products. The questions for implementation are, where do you find the proper applications, how do you complete the forms, where do you send the forms, and how do you attach any money to the application? **For investment and insurance, answers to these questions are on the internet and helpful personnel from the selected company are standing by to answer your questions.** Click on the company selected and follow the instructions on how to apply and process your application. Several sites to find suitable mutual funds include:

a. Vanguard.com
b. Fidellity.com
c. T-Roweprice.com
d. Schwab.com

In our example financial plan, three investment applications and one insurance application are required. Print a file copy of each completed application for your file.

Direct purchase insurance is purchased directly from the insurance company without paying any commissions. Term life insurance is pure protection; it is sold without a savings or investment component. Term insurance will only last until the end of the term, so it is not permanent. Conversely, whole life insurance is more expensive than term insurance, as some of the premiums are invested to build cash value. It is a permanent insurance and can be guaranteed for life.

Find the appropriate company website. Scroll to find the application process and follow the instructions. Investment applications are straight forward. Complete the application and attach the mode of payment like a check to open the mutual fund. Insurance applications take longer to complete. Your application will require medical, moral, and occupational questions. Answers to the questions will help determine your insurability and the rate classification for the cost of insurance. Preferred is the lowest-cost category of insurability. All applicants will not qualify for this preferred rating. Distractors that dictate a less-than-preferred rating are smoking, medical illness, hazardous occupation, or moral issues. Here, advice from an independent insurance agent can be very helpful. Don't become impatient with the process. It is the same process that you follow if you used a commissioned captive insurance agent to buy insurance. When you want and need to save commission cost, stay with our guidance.

Here are some of the direct insurance sites to surf in selecting your insurance company:

a. Select Quote.com
b. Direct General.com
c. Policygenius.com
d. AIG Direct.com
e. Massmutual.com
f. Mutualofomahalifeinsurance.com
g. New York Life.com

Chapter 5

Plan Review and Update

Your new do-it-yourself financial plan will not succeed unless it is reviewed and updated yearly. No one has ever accurately predicted stock market performance. This fact requires the planner to review the plan yearly to account for stock market results and any changes that the family might encounter during the year. Using the steps below will assist the planner to perform a complete review every year.

Plan Review:

1. Set the month and date to begin the review, then continue the review until complete. Perform the review the same month every year.
2. Record your beginning-year balances of each investments, 1 January.
3. Record the balance of each investment at year end, 30 December. Keep each year's confirmation statement per fund in file.
4. Calculate your investments' net rate of return. This is the result of all ending total balances minus all beginning total balances divided by the total beginning balances of all funds.
5. Compare your computed rate of return results to fund company result on the internet. This will validate your calculated rate of return.
6. Compare your calculated rate of return to the plans rate of return required to reach your goals, on time. You should use rate of return as your benchmark measurement for goal achievement. Comparing the rate of return required to accomplish goals to the yearly earned

rate of return will show if your investments are on track to achieve goals. When the compared rates of return are coequal or better, rejoice. When the achieved yearly rate of return is below 8%, additional monthly funding maybe required. In our example plan, the required investment monthly amount to reach goals is $2027 per month at 8% rate of return. Since we begin investing at $650 per month in our plan, periodic increases must be made until we reach the target $2027. The total goal of $3,021,151 divided by 1490.36 (monthly investing factor from compound interest table at 8% for 30 years) = $2,027 monthly dollars needed.

7. Review your insurance plan. Recall that our example family, the Rocksteady, did not execute final expense insurance for each member of the family. This required risk mitigation should be reviewed each year until purchased.

Plan Update:

1. Family changes cause the plan to be changed. A new child is born, the spouse going to work, and the breadwinner getting a pay raise are a few of the family changes that can require updates to the plan.
2. Plan review showing a less-than-needed rate of return during the review can be offset by adding monies to the plan.
3. Additional dollars available to invest due to pay raise or spouse going to work allows the family to fund planned increases to the plan to reach a glidepath that will achieve objectives.

The do-it-yourself planner that conducts the update must document the review of their work. Additionally, the planner must prepare a written narrative of the review/update with considerations for actions taken and not taken. File this narrative with all paperwork for use with next year's review.

Summary

Do-It-Yourself

This guide is a workable "how to" approach to achieving financial freedom via a simple financial plan. It is expressly written for those Americans that cannot afford a financial advisor and those Americans that do not know how to approach the objective of financial freedom. These instructions will save the do-it-yourself financial planner the cost of an advisor and firm, plus considerable savings on the cost of financial products. Over a lifetime, the savings will add up to thousands of dollars. Yet, the best approach to achieving financial independence, for those that can afford it, is through a professional financial advisor that will place the client first, ahead of firm and self. At least 50 percent of Americans cannot afford the cost of an advisor, firm, and brokered products. This does not have to be the case. Following the guidance of this book gives the do-it-yourself investor a low-cost, reasonable, workable, and simplistic method of achieving successful financial results.

Americans, regardless of income, desire financial success. It is the American dream. Investing available dollars yields the best and most powerful opportunity to make your money grow and work as hard as you do. Before publication of this guide, detailed investment instruction was just not available. Americans do not invest due to lack of know-how, lack of sufficient income, and the cost of acquiring professional financial planning and investing services. As the old saying goes, it is "high time" something is done about it. Make this strategy work for you. A wonderful and plentiful retirement awaits. My wish for you is good luck and much financial success.

Plan Tools

Risk Questionnaire

Instructions: Mark your response to questions 1 through 9, annotating your point score for each question. Total your scores for all 9 questions. Compare your total score to the risk categories of the risk allocation model located in planning tools. Your risk category will be conservative, moderate or aggressive."

1. I will start withdrawing money from my investment in:

                                                        Score

    - Less than 3 years (0)
    - 3 – 5 years (2)
    - 6 – 10 years (4)
    - 11 years or more (6)   _____

2. My knowledge of investments is described as:
    - None (0)
    - Limited (2)
    - Good (4)
    - Extensive (6)   _____

3. When investing my concern is:
    - Most concerned about losing investment value (0)
    - Equally concerned about losing or gaining value (3)
    - Most concerned about gaining value (6)

                                                                     _____

4. What if in the past three months the stock market lost 25% of its value and you lost 25% of your investment value? What would you do?
    - Sell all shares (0)
    - Sell some shares (2)
    - Do nothing (4)
    - Buy more shares (6)   _____

5. How secure is your income?
   - Not secure   (0)
   - Somewhat secure (2)
   - Fairly secure   (4)
   - Very secure   (6)   _____

6. What age range do you fall into?

	(Points)	Point Score
- Above 75	(1)	
- Between 66 and 75	(2)	
- Between 56 and 65	(3)	
- Between 46 and 55	(4)	
- Between 18 and 45	(5)	_____

7. Generally, I prefer investments with little or no fluctuation in value, and I am willing to accept the lower returns associated with these investments.
   - Strongly agree   (0)
   - Agree   (1)
   - Somewhat agree (3)
   - Disagree   (5)
   - Strongly disagree (6)   _____

8. I would invest in a mutual fund solely based on a brief conversation with a friend, colleague, or relative.
   - Strongly agree   (1)
   - Agree   (2)
   - Somewhat agree (3)
   - Disagree   (4)
   - Strongly disagree (5)   _____

9. Over a period of time, investments can rise and fall. This is called fluctuation. Generally, the higher the risk the higher the fluctuation. What level of fluctuation would you be comfortable with?
   - Between -5% and +5%   (1)
   - Between -10% and +10%   (2)
   - Between -15% and +15%   (3)
   - Between -20% and +20%   (4)
   - Between -25% and +25%   (5)   _____

Total Score: _____

Cash Flow Plan/Budget

Income	Monthly	Comments
Wages & Tips:		
Disability Income		
Specialty Pay/Overtime		
Bonus or Other Pay		
Rental Income		
Interest Income/Dividends		
Gifts Received		
Refunds/Reimbursements		
Other		
Other		
Other		
Total Income	$0.00	

Home Expenses	Monthly	Comments
Mortgage/Rent		
Home/Rental Insurance		
Electricity		
Gas/Oil		
Water/Sewer/Trash		
Phone		
Cable/Internet		
Internet		
Furnishings/Appliances		
Lawn/Garden		
Maintenance/Supplies		
Improvements		
Other - Condo Fee		
Total Home Expenses		

Transportation	Monthly	Comments
Vehicle Payments		
Auto Insurance		
Fuel		
Bus/Taxi/Train Fare		
Repairs		
Rental Income		
Registration/License		
Total Transportation		

Health	Monthly	Comments
Health Savings Account		
Flex Spending Account		
Health Insurance		
Doctor/Dentist		
Medicine/Drugs		
Health Club Dues		
Veterinarian/Pet Care		
Other		
Total Health		

Charity/Gifts	Monthly	Comments
Gifts Given		
Charitable Donations		
Religious Donations/Tithe		
Other		
Total Charity/Gifts		

Subscriptions	Monthly	Comments
Newspaper		
Magazines		
Dues/Memberships		
Other		
Total Subscriptions		

Taxes & Debts	Monthly	Comment
Federal Taxes		
Federal Taxes		
Social Security (OASDI)		
Social Security (OASDI)		
State/Local Taxes		
State/Local Taxes		
Personal Loan/Consolidation Loan		
Credit Card(s)		
Student Loan(s)		
TSP/401K Loan		
Alimony/Child Support		
Total Daily Living		

Entertainment	Monthly	Comments
Vacation/Travel		
Hobbies/Sports		
Music/Games/Rental/Books		
Outdoor Recreation		
Toys/Gadgets		
Movies/Theater/Concert/Plays		
Other/Misc.		
Total Entertainment		

Financial Planning	Monthly	Comments
Emergency Fund/Savings		
Pay Cash Account (for goals)		
Non-Employer Life Insurance		
Employer Life Insurance		
Retirement (401k, TSP, IRAs)		
IRA Investments (Trad/Roth)		
Non-IRA Investments (SR/Joint/Trust)		
College Accounts (529/ESA/UGMA)		
Long Term Care (LTC)		
Disability Insurance (S/L Term)		
Financial Planning Fee/Expense		
Tax Profissional Fee		
Estate Planning Expense		
Total Financial Planning		

Daily Living	Monthly	Comments
Groceries		
Personal Supplies		
Clothing/Upkeep		
Cleaning		
Education/Lessons		
Dining/Eating Out		
Salon/Barber		
Pet Food		
Total Obligations		

Miscellaneous	Monthly	Comments
Bank Fees		
Postage		
Pet Insurance		
Other		
Total Miscellaneous		

Monthly Budget Summary	Monthly	Comments
Total Income		
Total Expenses		
Total Unallocated/NET		

Risk Allocation Model

- Risk averse - Seeking more stable investment returns over time	- Comfortable with a moderate level of risk - Seeking a balance between risk and return	- Able to tolerate significant market fluctuation and risk - Seeking to maximize capital growth over time
Conservative Risk	**Moderate Risk**	**Aggressive Risk**
- 20% allocation to stock to reduce risk exposure - 80% allocation to Cash/Bonds	- 50% allocation to stocks to gain modest capital growth potential - 50% allocation to Bonds	- 80% *allocation to stock to maximize capital* growth - 20% allocation to Bonds

RISK SCORE: 0-20	**RISK SCORE: 21-35**	**RISK SCORE: 36-51**
20% 80% ■ Stocks ■ Cash/Bonds	50% 50% ■ Stocks ■ Bonds	20% 80% ■ Stocks ■ Bonds

MONTHLY COMPOUND INTEREST TABLES

8.00% ANNUAL INTEREST RATE   0.6667% MONTHLY EFFECTIVE INTEREST RATE

	1 AMOUNT OF $1 AT COMPOUND INTEREST	2 ACCUMULATION OF $1 PER PERIOD	3 SINKING FUND FACTOR	4 PRESENT VALUE REVERSION OF $1	5 PRESENT VALUE ORD. ANNUITY $1 PER PERIOD	6 INSTALLMENT TO AMORTIZE $1	
MONTHS							MONTHS
1	1.006667	1.000000	1.000000	0.993377	0.993377	1.006667	1
2	1.013378	2.006667	0.498339	0.986799	1.980176	0.505006	2
3	1.020134	3.020044	0.331121	0.980264	2.960440	0.337788	3
4	1.026935	4.040178	0.247514	0.973772	3.934212	0.254181	4
5	1.033781	5.067113	0.197351	0.967323	4.901535	0.204018	5
6	1.040673	6.100893	0.163910	0.960917	5.862452	0.170577	6
7	1.047610	7.141546	0.140025	0.954553	6.817005	0.146692	7
8	1.054595	8.189176	0.122112	0.948232	7.765237	0.128779	8
9	1.061625	9.243771	0.108181	0.941952	8.707189	0.114848	9
10	1.068703	10.305396	0.097037	0.935714	9.642903	0.103703	10
11	1.075827	11.374099	0.087919	0.929517	10.572420	0.094586	11
12	1.083000	12.449926	0.080322	0.923361	11.495782	0.086988	12
YEARS							MONTHS
1	1.083000	12.449926	0.080322	0.923361	11.495782	0.086988	12
2	1.172888	25.933190	0.038561	0.852596	22.110544	0.045227	24
3	1.270237	40.535558	0.024670	0.787255	31.911806	0.031336	36
4	1.375666	56.349915	0.017746	0.726921	40.961913	0.024413	48
5	1.489846	73.476856	0.013610	0.671210	49.318433	0.020276	60
6	1.613502	92.025325	0.010867	0.619770	57.034522	0.017533	72
7	1.747422	112.113308	0.008920	0.572272	64.159261	0.015586	84
8	1.892457	133.868583	0.007470	0.528414	70.737970	0.014137	96
9	2.049530	157.429535	0.006352	0.487917	76.812497	0.013019	108
10	2.219640	182.946035	0.005466	0.450523	82.421481	0.012133	120
11	2.403869	210.580392	0.004749	0.415996	87.600600	0.011415	132
12	2.603389	240.508387	0.004158	0.384115	92.382800	0.010825	144
13	2.819469	272.920390	0.003664	0.354677	96.798498	0.010331	156
14	3.053484	308.022574	0.003247	0.327495	100.875784	0.009913	168
15	3.306921	346.038222	0.002890	0.302396	104.640592	0.009557	180
16	3.581394	387.209149	0.002583	0.279221	108.116871	0.009249	192
17	3.878648	431.797244	0.002316	0.257822	111.326733	0.008983	204
18	4.200574	480.086128	0.002083	0.238063	114.290596	0.008750	216
19	4.549220	532.382966	0.001878	0.219818	117.027313	0.008545	228
20	4.926803	589.020416	0.001698	0.202971	119.554292	0.008364	240
21	5.335725	650.358746	0.001538	0.187416	121.887606	0.008204	252
22	5.778588	716.788127	0.001395	0.173053	124.042099	0.008062	264
23	6.258207	788.731114	0.001268	0.159790	126.031475	0.007935	276
24	6.777636	866.645333	0.001154	0.147544	127.868388	0.007821	288
25	7.340176	951.026395	0.001051	0.136237	129.564523	0.007718	300
26	7.949407	1042.411042	0.000959	0.125796	131.130668	0.007626	312
27	8.609204	1141.380571	0.000876	0.116155	132.576786	0.007543	324
28	9.323763	1248.564521	0.000801	0.107253	133.912076	0.007468	336
29	10.097631	1364.644687	0.000733	0.099033	135.145031	0.007399	348
30	10.935730	1490.359449	0.000671	0.091443	136.283494	0.007338	360
31	11.843390	1626.508474	0.000615	0.084435	137.334707	0.007281	372
32	12.826385	1773.957801	0.000564	0.077964	138.305357	0.007230	384
33	13.890969	1933.645350	0.000517	0.071989	139.201617	0.007184	396
34	15.043913	2106.586886	0.000475	0.066472	140.029190	0.007141	408
35	16.292550	2293.882485	0.000436	0.061378	140.793338	0.007103	420
36	17.644824	2496.723526	0.000401	0.056674	141.498923	0.007067	432
37	19.109335	2716.400273	0.000368	0.052330	142.150433	0.007035	444
38	20.695401	2954.310082	0.000338	0.048320	142.752013	0.007005	456
39	22.413109	3211.966288	0.000311	0.044617	143.307488	0.006978	468
40	24.273386	3491.007831	0.000286	0.041197	143.820392	0.006953	480

	Single Payment		Uniform Payment Series				Arithmetic Gradient		
	Compound Amount Factor Find F Given P F/P	Present Worth Factor Find P Given F P/F	Sinking Fund Factor Find A Given F A/F	Capital Recovery Factor Find A Given P A/P	Compound Amount Factor Find F Given A F/A	Present Worth Factor Find P Given A P/A	Gradient Uniform Series Find A Given G A/G	Gradient Present Worth Find P Given G P/G	
n									n
1	1.030	.9709	1.0000	1.0300	1.000	0.971	0	0	1
2	1.061	.9426	.4926	.5226	2.030	1.913	0.493	0.943	2
3	1.093	.9151	.3235	.3535	3.091	2.829	0.980	2.773	3
4	1.126	.8885	.2390	.2690	4.184	3.717	1.463	5.438	4
5	1.159	.8626	.1884	.2184	5.309	4.580	1.941	8.889	5
6	1.194	.8375	.1546	.1846	6.468	5.417	2.414	13.076	6
7	1.230	.8131	.1305	.1605	7.662	6.230	2.882	17.955	7
8	1.267	.7894	.1125	.1425	8.892	7.020	3.345	23.481	8
9	1.305	.7664	.0984	.1284	10.159	7.786	3.803	29.612	9
10	1.344	.7441	.0872	.1172	11.464	8.530	4.256	36.309	10
11	1.384	.7224	.0781	.1081	12.808	9.253	4.705	43.533	11
12	1.426	.7014	.0705	.1005	14.192	9.954	5.148	51.248	12
13	1.469	.6810	.0640	.0940	15.618	10.635	5.587	59.419	13
14	1.513	.6611	.0585	.0885	17.086	11.296	6.021	68.014	14
15	1.558	.6419	.0538	.0838	18.599	11.938	6.450	77.000	15
16	1.605	.6232	.0496	.0796	20.157	12.561	6.874	86.348	16
17	1.653	.6050	.0460	.0760	21.762	13.166	7.294	96.028	17
18	1.702	.5874	.0427	.0727	23.414	13.754	7.708	106.014	18
19	1.754	.5703	.0398	.0698	25.117	14.324	8.118	116.279	19
20	1.806	.5537	.0372	.0672	26.870	14.877	8.523	126.799	20
21	1.860	.5375	.0349	.0649	28.676	15.415	8.923	137.549	21
22	1.916	.5219	.0327	.0627	30.537	15.937	9.319	148.509	22
23	1.974	.5067	.0308	.0608	32.453	16.444	9.709	159.656	23
24	2.033	.4919	.0290	.0590	34.426	16.936	10.095	170.971	24
25	2.094	.4776	.0274	.0574	36.459	17.413	10.477	182.433	25
26	2.157	.4637	.0259	.0559	38.553	17.877	10.853	194.026	26
27	2.221	.4502	.0246	.0546	40.710	18.327	11.226	205.731	27
28	2.288	.4371	.0233	.0533	42.931	18.764	11.593	217.532	28
29	2.357	.4243	.0221	.0521	45.219	19.188	11.956	229.413	29
30	2.427	.4120.	.0210	.0510	47.575	19.600	12.314	241.361	30
31	2.500	.4000	.0200	.0500	50.003	20.000	12.668	253.361	31
32	2.575	.3883	.0190	.0490	52.503	20.389	13.017	265.399	32
33	2.652	.3770	.0182	.0482	55.078	20.766	13.362	277.464	33
34	2.732	.3660	.0173	.0473	57.730	21.132	13.702	289.544	34
35	2.814	.3554	.0165	.0465	60.462	21.487	14.037	301.627	35
40	3.262	.3066	.0133	.0433	75.401	23.115	15.650	361.750	40
45	3.782	.2644	.0108	.0408	92.720	24.519	17.156	420.632	45
50	4.384	.2281	.00887	.0389	112.797	25.730	18.558	477.480	50
55	5.082	.1968	.00735	.0373	136.072	26.774	19.860	531.741	55
60	5.892	.1697	.00613	.0361	163.053	27.676	21.067	583.052	60
65	6.830	.1464	.00515	.0351	194.333	28.453	22.184	631.201	65
70	7.918	.1263	.00434	.0343	230.594	29.123	23.215	676.087	70
75	9.179	.1089	.00367	.0337	272.631	29.702	24.163	717.698	75
80	10.641	.0940	.00311	.0331	321.363	30.201	25.035	756.086	80
85	12.336	.0811	.00265	.0326	377.857	30.631	25.835	791.353	85
90	14.300	.0699	.00226	.0323	443.349	31.002	26.567	823.630	90
95	16.578	.0603	.00193	.0319	519.272	31.323	27.235	853.074	95
100	19.219	.0520	.00165	.0316	607.287	31.599	27.844	879.854	100

	Single Payment		Uniform Payment Series				Arithmetic Gradient		
	Compound Amount Factor Find F Given P F/P	Present Worth Factor Find P Given F P/F	Sinking Fund Factor Find A Given F A/F	Capital Recovery Factor Find A Given P A/P	Compound Amount Factor Find F Given A F/A	Present Worth Factor Find P Given A P/A	Gradient Uniform Series Find A Given G A/G	Gradient Present Worth Find P Given G P/G	n
n									
1	1.080	.9259	1.0000	1.0800	1.000	0.926	0	0	1
2	1.166	.8573	.4808	.5608	2.080	1.783	0.481	0.857	2
3	1.260	.7938	.3080	.3880	3.246	2.577	0.949	2.445	3
4	1.360	.7350	.2219	.3019	4.506	3.312	1.404	4.650	4
5	1.469	.6806	.1705	.2505	5.867	3.993	1.846	7.372	5
6	1.587	.6302	.1363	.2163	7.336	4.623	2.276	10.523	6
7	1.714	.5835	.1121	.1921	8.923	5.206	2.694	14.024	7
8	1.851	.5403	.0940	.1740	10.637	5.747	3.099	17.806	8
9	1.999	.5002	.0801	.1601	12.488	6.247	3.491	21.808	9
10	2.159	.4632	.0690	.1490	14.487	6.710	3.871	25.977	10
11	2.332	.4289	.0601	.1401	16.645	7.139	4.240	30.266	11
12	2.518	.3971	.0527	.1327	18.977	7.536	4.596	34.634	12
13	2.720	.3677	.0465	.1265	21.495	7.904	4.940	39.046	13
14	2.937	.3405	.0413	.1213	24.215	8.244	5.273	43.472	14
15	3.172	.3152	.0368	.1168	27.152	8.559	5.594	47.886	15
16	3.426	.2919	.0330	.1130	30.324	8.851	5.905	52.264	16
17	3.700	.2703	.0296	.1096	33.750	9.122	6.204	56.588	17
18	3.996	.2502	.0267	.1067	37.450	9.372	6.492	60.843	18
19	4.316	.2317	.0241	.1041	41.446	9.604	6.770	65.013	19
20	4.661	.2145	.0219	.1019	45.762	9.818	7.037	69.090	20
21	5.034	.1987	.0198	.0998	50.423	10.017	7.294	73.063	21
22	5.437	.1839	.0180	.0980	55.457	10.201	7.541	76.926	22
23	5.871	.1703	.0164	.0964	60.893	10.371	7.779	80.673	23
24	6.341	.1577	.0150	.0950	66.765	10.529	8.007	84.300	24
25	6.848	.1460	.0137	.0937	73.106	10.675	8.225	87.804	25
26	7.396	.1352	.0125	.0925	79.954	10.810	8.435	91.184	26
27	7.988	.1252	.0114	.0914	87.351	10.935	8.636	94.439	27
28	8.627	.1159	.0105	.0905	95.339	11.051	8.829	97.569	28
29	9.317	.1073	.00962	.0896	103.966	11.158	9.013	100.574	29
30	10.063	.0994	.00883	.0888	113.283	11.258	9.190	103.456	30
31	10.868	.0920	.00811	.0881	123.346	11.350	9.358	106.216	31
32	11.737	.0852	.00745	.0875	134.214	11.435	9.520	108.858	32
33	12.676	.0789	.00685	.0869	145.951	11.514	9.674	111.382	33
34	13.690	.0730	.00630	.0863	158.627	11.587	9.821	113.792	34
35	14.785	.0676	.00580	.0858	172.317	11.655	9.961	116.092	35
40	21.725	.0460	.00386	.0839	259.057	11.925	10.570	126.042	40
45	31.920	.0313	.00259	.0826	386.506	12.108	11.045	133.733	45
50	46.902	.0213	.00174	.0817	573.771	12.233	11.411	139.593	50
55	68.914	.0145	.00118	.0812	848.925	12.319	11.690	144.006	55
60	101.257	.00988	.00080	.0808	1 253.2	12.377	11.902	147.300	60
65	148.780	.00672	.00054	.0805	1 847.3	12.416	12.060	149.739	65
70	218.607	.00457	.00037	.0804	2 720.1	12.443	12.178	151.533	70
75	321.205	.00311	.00025	.0802	4 002.6	12.461	12.266	152.845	75
80	471.956	.00212	.00017	.0802	5 887.0	12.474	12.330	153.800	80
85	693.458	.00144	.00012	.0801	8 655.7	12.482	12.377	154.492	85
90	1 018.9	.00098	.00008	.0801	12 724.0	12.488	12.412	154.993	90
95	1 497.1	.00067	.00005	.0801	18 701.6	12.492	12.437	155.352	95
100	2 199.8	.00045	.00004	.0800	27 484.6	12.494	12.455	155.611	100